The Military Transition Challenge: Essential Perspectives for Civilian Career Positioning

Dr. David P. Peltz

Disclaimer

The information provided within this book is for general informational purposes only. While we try to keep the information up-to-date and correct, there are no representations or warranties, express or implied, about the completeness, accuracy, reliability, suitability or availability with respect to the information, products, services, or related graphics contained in this eBook for any purpose. Any use of this information is at your own risk. If you wish to apply ideas contained in this book, you are taking full responsibility for your actions.

The methods describe within this book are the author's personal thoughts. They are not intended to be a definitive set of instructions for this project. You may discover there are other methods and materials to accomplish the same end result.

The author has made every effort to ensure the accuracy of the information within this book was correct at time of publication. The author does not assume and hereby disclaims any liability to any party for any loss, damage, or disruption caused by errors or omissions, whether such errors or omissions result from accident, negligence, or any other cause.

ISBN: 1546516352
ISBN-13: 978-1546516354

CONTENTS

DR. DAVID P. PELTZ

ACKNOWLEDGMENTS

Thank you to my wife, Julie, and son, David, for their constant love and support. Because of them, I am always striving to achieve more.

Thank you to my parents, family, friends, and colleagues for their unconditional and unwavering support.

Thank you to all the men and women serving and who have served our great nation. We are a great nation because of your vigilance, service, and sacrifice.

PREFACE

READ THIS FIRST: The Way this Book is Written

This book is intended to provide you (active, reserve, guard, or veteran) with a degree of awareness and detail that will enable you to better position yourself in your transition to from military to civilian status. In effect, you are learning to become a civilian. While the overall tone of this book is geared towards military members and veterans, the principles and concepts throughout can also be applied to the general public (aka. civilians). The approach is based upon nearly 25 years of personal and professional anecdotal experiences and observations. It is never too late to apply the information contained within these pages. The goal is to furnish you with a basic understanding that will help assist you in positioning yourself for a successful career outside the military. Several concepts, principles, and strategies will be discussed throughout this four-part book.

Many of you will want to skip this section and go straight to Part IV of this book to read the practical tips…PLEASE DO NOT SKIP TO PART IV. This guidebook is divided into four parts: premise, strategic, tactical, and practical. Each section provides a fundamental basis for the one that follows. Think of it as building a house…you need the plans first, then the foundation and framing, roof, and finally the interior finishes. We need to build from the ground up.

To ensure we gain the MOST insightful advantage, we need to have a solid understanding of what is challenging us. In military history, very few battles and wars have been won by simply running in to a situation blindly. In this short guidebook, we will explore several of the personal and professional challenges of transitioning from military to civilian status. Over the past several years, I have made observations from posting trends online, discussions with my college students, talking with peers and colleagues, and listening to transitioning and/or prior military members expressing consternation on becoming a new civilian, or those returning to civilian status. Posts, articles, and discussions have originated from officers and enlisted, retiring and general separation, college educated and non-degreed, male and female members, and all ethnic backgrounds.

My empathy, sympathy, gratitude, and support goes out to each of you embarking on this next phase in your life journey, and I cannot thank you enough for your service, dedication, and sacrifice you have made to our nation and country, and its eternally grateful people. Let it be acknowledged, new and exciting (and often frustrating) challenges await you. There are however, a few things you can do in preparation to make this transition "easier". I have transitioned from military to civilian status three different times. What this means is I have had three opportunities to learn and identify key elements for successfully transitioning from the military to civilian status. What I learned was having a team at my side made the learning curve much less steep. During my transitions, I inevitably found myself taking the long scenic route versus the direct flight to my destination of civilian status. It also enabled me to learn the many positive and frustrating nuances of the military to civilian transition. I never failed at transitioning because I was always learning – I repeated the things that worked well, and did not repeat the things that had less than desirable results. I viewed each transition as an opportunity to obtain a greater level of understanding and expertise in how to successfully transition from a military to civilian environment. Each time became easier in some ways, yet was more challenging in others.

OPERATIONAL DEFINITIONS

position
1. A place or location.
2. A strategic area occupied by members of a force.
4. An advantageous place or location.
5. A situation as it relates to the surrounding circumstances.
6. A point of view or attitude on a certain question.
(American Heritage® Dictionary of the English Language, Fifth Edition)

perspective
1. a way of regarding situations, facts, etc, and judging their relative importance
2. the proper or accurate point of view or the ability to see it; objectivity
(Collins English Dictionary– Complete and Unabridged, 12th Edition)

perception
1. the act or faculty of apprehending by means of the senses or the mind; cognition; awareness.
2. a single unified awareness derived from sensory processes while a stimulus is present.
3. immediate or intuitive recognition or appreciation, as of moral, psychological, or aesthetic qualities; insight; discernment.
4. the result or product of perceiving; percept.
(Random House Kernerman Webster's College Dictionary)

PART I: THE PREMISE FOR THIS BOOK

1. Your New Beginning!
   i. The Transition Challenge Question
   ii. Clarification: I am not a Pastry Chef
   iii. The Military to Civilian Transition Experience

2. Who I am to You…We are Very Similar, You and I
   i. Formative Years
   ii. Military Career
   iii. Civilian Career
   iv. Education
   v. Military, Civilian, Education Journey Timeline

1 YOUR NEW BEGINNING!

The Transition Challenge Question

A question for you to ponder is: Will you take the long scenic road; or the shorter more direct route? Much can be said about each option. The long scenic road will allow you to gain a vast about knowledge, experience, and wisdom. The shorter more direct route will allow you to gain from the knowledge, experience, and wisdom of others. There will always be those that want to experience things for themselves…and that is fine. However, in this, your new beginning, life will be just as competitive and time sensitive as it was in the military…perhaps even more so.

Clarification: I am not a Pastry Chef

To provide a little clarity, let me state for the

record, I have been there and done that – three times (more on this shortly). I do know what you will/may go through and experience during your transition; and I know how to get through it. Additionally, you may not like what I will say at times, but it will be the truth and/or my professional opinion. I will be straight forward with you – I will not sugar coat anything; hence I am not a pastry chef.

The Military to Civilian Transition Experience

You will be filled with a plethora of emotional and psychological ups and downs as you transition – sorry no way around this one. There will be times of extreme joy, happiness, satisfaction, and accomplishment. Unfortunately, you will also, encounter the polar opposites to these emotions. This is completely normal, and is part of the de-institutionalization process. Yes, that is correct, you have been institutionalized to the ways of the military. The first thing do is to accept that this is a normal developmental phase, and then rely upon your military training on how to deal with stressful situations (i.e. remain calm and collected, and start developing a plan).

2 WHO I AM TO YOU...WE ARE VERY SIMILAR, YOU AND I

Throughout my career, many people have shared their life's woes with me. They attributed those woes as the reasons why they have not been able to accomplish certain personal and professional goals. Despite the proverbial military 'crap sandwiches' we are served throughout our lives and careers, we CAN make a series of conscious choices to overcome any challenge or obstacle we encounter. Regardless of rank, position, gender, religion, socio-economic status, education level, upbringing, etc., we all bleed the same color, and are human beings capable of conscious choice and compassion. I share the following candid life experiences with you to show I too have been served my share of crap sandwiches. Yet, I was able to use those experiences to help me overcome all of the challenges I encountered throughout my life. I have provided a degree of transparency in my life event summaries. As you will see, while reading this section, it is likely you and I have much in common.

Formative Years

Family divorce. I am a child of divorce (a couple times over). I am not totally convinced I should lead with this because it is virtually a socially accepted norm to come from a family of divorce. Perhaps most interesting about this fact is not only did my parents divorce, but they remarried and divorced again, and then remarried for a final time. I will say, in both cases, I was grateful for the second divorce as my first set of step parents were rather awful and abusive, conservatively speaking. For many years, this abuse had a lasting effect on my self-image and confidence. On the flip side, both of my current step parents (for many decades) are as wonderful as step parents come, and both have been pillars in my overall development and growth over the years. A little love, compassion, and support can go a very long way.

Moving a lot. To say I moved many times and attended lots of schools would be an understatement to some. From kindergarten through high school, I attended 10 different schools. The least amount of time I spent at one school was one semester (four semesters, back to back); during sixth and seventh grades, I attended four different schools. The longest time at one school was three years. During high school, I attended two schools, and the last three years were at the same school. Because I was the habitual "new kid" at each school I attended, bullies tended to gravitate towards me…like they could smell the "new kid" fear in me or something. The repetition of moving provided me with the ability to adapt to new and ever changing environments. I also learned perseverance…and of course, how to pack suitcases and boxes EXTREMELY well, and fast.

Poor grades. Let us talk about my grades in high school for a moment. My high school GPA was nothing to brag about (a C: 2.6 GPA). I had to take a couple of extra night school classes my senior year just to have enough credits to graduate because I had failed several courses my first two years of high school. The only reason my GPA was as high as it was, was because I took several art classes my last two years of school and it boosted my overall GPA from a D+/C-to the mid-C range. A good student, I was not, unless it was an art class. What I would later learn was that having poor grades in high school did not have to dictate how I would perform in college.

Military Career

During my enlisted military service, I was in the Security Police/Security Forces in the U.S. Air Force, U.S. Air Force Reserve, and Arizona Air National Guard. I served six years on active duty during the first Gulf War, about 2.5 years in the reserves, and three years in the national guard. During the latter half of my national guard service, I was activated for the second Gulf War. Each time I was in the military, I had a break in service of a couple years in between. During my first enlistment in the U.S. Air Force, I was stationed in The Netherlands, and then in Minot,

North Dakota. During my time in the U.S. Air Force Reserve, I was assigned in Phoenix, Arizona. While in the Arizona Air National Guard serving on active duty as a part of the second Gulf war, I was injured off duty and received an involuntary honorable discharge under medical conditions. That was my second honorable discharge. I was an E-5, had been in the military for a total of 11.5 years, and accumulated nearly 10 years of active service. I was frustrated, upset, and felt left behind by the military I loved and served. I served in three different capacities of the military, all in the Security Police/Security Forces field. If I am being completely honest, it was a bit of a love/hate relationship (as many of us can attest). But the fact I served in the military on three different occasions means I also had to transition from military to civilian status three times. Those transitions became the catalyst for my journeys and experiences in military transitioning and career positioning.

Civilian Career

My civilian career can be divided into three basic categories: state corrections; corporate (retail management, college enrollment advisor, DOD/defense, technology sector); and consulting and higher education. I will not bore you with the details but will say that during my time in state corrections I was in the U.S. Air Force Reserve, and that my consulting and higher education overlapped my time in the defense and IT sectors. The reason this is important is because it shows strategic foresight and planning. I had a plan and was sticking to it. I also had a backup plan, a plan that would later be crucial to my success.

Education

In my formative years, I did not view myself as smart, in fact it was just the opposite, my first set of step parents made sure I understood that I would not amount to anything and that I was just another dumb/stupid snot-nosed child in the world. While in the U.S. Air Force Reserve (and working for state corrections), one of my military colleagues who was in college (we will call him Sergeant D.B.) talked to me about starting college. He helped me realize I <u>was</u> smart; smart enough to attend college. I was so inspired by him, I started the next semester at community college. I went on to earn a Bachelor's degree with a Business Management major, then an Master's degree in business with a Global Management specialization; and eventually earned a Doctorate of philosophy in Organizational Leadership with a Human Resource Development major.

Military, Civilian, Education Journey Timeline

Synapsis. I have made the transition from military to civilian three times in my career. The first time was in 1993, the second was in 1997, the third and last was in 2003. What I learned from each of my experiences, and through talking with others (enlisted and officer) was that rank and the year of separation did not matter…experientially, the transition challenges were very similar and/or even identical.

First military term. During my first separation, I was a non-commissioned officer (NCO) and it was during the involuntary reduction in force period in the Clinton administration. Due to my low time in service and time in grade, I would have to score 98% or better on both my promotional exams – something that was virtually unheard of. Per Air Force policy, scoring a 98% or better on either exam, would automatically trigger an investigation for cheating and required repeating the test(s). To put things into perspective, the average test scores at the time were in the mid 80's with the occasional very low 90's. I was in a precarious position whereby if I reenlisted I would be in the military on a week to week basis until I was able to promote. So, I opted to get out of the military "on my own terms". I did not adjust well to civilian life; I missed the mission, responsibility, comradery, and serving our country. Over the course of the following year I wrote letters requesting to be to return to active duty and sent them through the entire the chain of command, up to and including the Joint Chief of Staff. My requests were all denied. I learned that sometimes change is inevitable and took it as an opportunity to grow.

Second military term. During my second transition from military to civilian status, I was still an NCO and I was working at the state prison (to clarify: as an employee, not an inmate). The prison management staff did not like their corrections officers and supervisors being in the military. When they found out you were in the reserves or guard, they would make your work schedule a virtual nightmare by deliberately scheduling you to work over the

9

weekends forcing you to use your vacation and paid time off during your drill weekends and annual trainings. This effectively left you with no time off for the year and working from three to six weeks in a row without any days off. If we did not use our vacation/paid time off for our drill weekends (or ran out of time off), we would be marked as a no call/no show/absent from post without approval. I was released from the reserves due to the financial hardship I was incurring from the 3.5-hour commute to the base and having run out of vacation time to "cover" my state corrections shifts. This transition was a bit more palatable because I was losing money and working endless shifts without very many days off each month. However, I still felt as if I had been ousted after being ostracized by management for being in the military. I took away from this experience my continued love of service to our country, and expertise in behavioral awareness in extreme environments and situations.

Third military term. My third transition was also very difficult. I felt I had finally made it back into the military for good – after all, the third time is the charm, and I had planned to retire from the military. I was in college, on active duty orders from the guard for the U.S. Air Force during the second gulf war, and the U.S. Air Force had just come out with an incentive program for enlisted members to cross over into the commissioned medical administration field – the incentive was to have O3 (Captain) in three years versus the standard five to six years. I was about a year out from finishing my bachelor's degree when I was involved in an off-duty accident (not a cool or sexy accident either – unless, that is, falling off a tall wood fence is cool or sexy) that crushed my right ankle and broke my tibia and fibula – nothing but the skin holding my foot to my leg, it was bad. I felt as if all my plans had been shattered. Just over a year later I received my second honorable discharge, this one under medical conditions. I left the military angry at the system, and upset, disappointed, and frustrated. I felt like the military had turned its back on me…essentially saying "you are broken, go sit on the bench, we do not want you to play anymore". The silver lining here was the month and year I received my second honorable discharge was at the same month and year I graduated from college with my bachelor's degree (which also happened to be my back up plan).

Segue. Up to this point in the book, it has been a lot about me and my experiences, albeit rather tersely summarized. This has been a fundamentally developed foundation to establish a baseline of trust to help you to understand that while I had three transition "do-overs", each experience was different, with its own nuances and frustrations. Additionally, you do not have to transition alone as I did – three times – without any help, assistance, or guidance from others who had transitioned before me.

PART II: STRATEGIC PERSPECTIVES

3 UNDERSTANDING MOTIVATION

To be truly successful in navigating the military transition challenge, we must have a solid underpinning of our current situation. This section includes several fundamental psycho-social elements intended to provide a clearer understanding of our current situation, and from whence the experientially based information has been sourced. These are the underpinning strategic elements for a successful transition.

We need to understand that there are two primary types of motivation. The two types of motivation I am referring to are NOT: "Do as I say, not as I do!" and "Drop down and give me 20!" . Motivation, from a theoretical lens, is divided into two high level categories: intrinsic motivation and extrinsic motivation.

Significance of Motivation

Why is understanding motivation important? It is important because it helps us to understand why we do the things we do, and why they are important to us. It helps us to put into perspective the "why" aspect of why we like/dislike or love/not love or feel obligated/not obligated to serve in the military. We all voluntarily signed up to serve in the military; we chose to serve. The question then becomes why did we sign up to serve in the military? Then followed by, which type of motivation do we most associate with for serving in the military? Once we understand the motivational aspect, we can begin to acknowledge and unravel the source of our frustration, angst, loss, happiness, celebration, achievement, etc. These, in turn, give insight into what we are feeling, thinking, or experiencing regarding our separation from the military.

Intrinsic Motivation (Deci, 1975; Deci & Ryan, 1985)

Intrinsic motivation is essentially doing something or engaging in an activity because that activity brings you joy. In other words, you do it because you love doing it. A couple of personal examples are, I like do-it-yourself (DIY) home improvement projects, puttering around with my performance car, and drawing with charcoal pencils. Professionally, I like mentoring military members and veterans, teaching college, and serving a greater cause (like the military).

Extrinsic Motivation (Vroom, 1964)

Extrinsic motivation is doing something or engaging in an activity to achieve and/or receive something (or not receive something). Examples of this include receiving a promotion and/or pay raise (whatever those elusive things are, am I right?), gaining recognition, receiving a gift/prize/award, attaining a higher functional position, having more clout and credibility, or job security. Conversely, it could also be engaging in an activity so you do not receive something: e.g., a punishment, demotion, fine, penalty, doing more push-ups etc. Simply stated, you can think of extrinsic motivation as form of quid pro quo; this for that.

4 INSTITUTIONALIZATION

If you start to reading this section and find yourself saying/thinking "I am not institutionalized to the military", then you are DEFINITELY institutionalized to the military. It is an inherent fact of being in the military. It (the military way of life) began in basic training and has been reinforced repeatedly over the years throughout your entire military service and career. See, you have been intentionally institutionalized – boo-ya!

Defining Institutionalization:

institutionalize

1. To make into, treat as, or give the character of an institution to: "The Irish institutionalized their language, requiring it on official documents" (Mark Abley).

18

2. To place (a person) in the care of an institution. (www.thefreedictionary.com/institutionalization)

Effectively, you were placed into an environment (in other words, "institution") where a specific set of beliefs, behaviors, and expectations were culturally reinforced to the degree of becoming accepted as a common social/societal/cultural norm.

Prime Examples of Institutionalization

Yes, you are institutionalized/conditioned (to what degree is the question). If you are still uncertain or doubting the fact you have been institutionalized to the military environment/culture, below are 10 examples affirming a few of the elemental aspects of cultural conditioning you have experienced throughout your military service.

1.   Military basic training
2.   Military technical schools
3.   Military leadership schools
4.   Military culture/life
5.   Military social reinforcement/events
6.   Military expectations
7.   Military leadership examples/behaviors
8.   Military promotions
9.   Military recognitions
10. Military awards

In the case of the military, you voluntarily entered the military environment, which further facilitated the acceptance of the culturally accepted societal norms. This is a good thing, as it assisted you in the adaption of this new environment. The same attitude of acceptance towards your new civilian environment will aid you in your military to civilian transition.

5 ALTERING YOUR PERSPECTIVE

Perspective is all about objectivity and conscious choice. What decisions, attitudes, perceptions, and ideas you use to adopt a given perspective is all about the choices you make. You choose your perspectives; therefore, you can choose to alter your perspectives. Altering one's perspective can provide very valuable insights about our surroundings. Phrases such as "thinking outside the box" or "taking a third person view" or "what would Jesus do" or "what would your parents/best friend say" all come to mind. They each evoke the mental side step from our current/present situation and challenge us to think about, and potentially approach, the situation from a different angle. Just like in the military when we are faced with a challenging task, we mentally assess the task and formulate a plan of attack. Sometimes this plan requires us to approach the situation using an alternate/creative method that may/may not have been used before. The same holds true regarding taking an alternate perspective towards our transition from military to civilian status.

Insanity = doing the same thing repeatedly and expecting a different result (Albert Einstein)

This is also on my all-time favorites list of perspective altering approaches. It tells us to step back and reassess our approach towards an event/a situation. We saw this circumstance unfold over and over, and time and time again, in basic training when one person would repeatedly do the same thing then have this perplexed look on their face when the drill instructor would have them do yet another set of push-ups/sit-ups/laps. Simply stated, if what you are doing is not working...change what you are doing...break the cycle...start anew...approach it from a different angle. We (humans) are habitual beings. The military emphasizes to us that we should alter our routines regularly. This is a learned military survival technique. Not only does it force us to be unpredictable, it challenges us to develop alternate approaches and solutions to our environment/situation.

Permanent Change in Perspective (PCP)

Yes, it will be like the drug (but with no associated brain damage-just an occasional headache).

Yes, at first, it will be euphoric, and confusing, with moments of intense clarity, followed by periods of confounding consternation.

There will also be an emotional crash a short time after you separate from the military, when you come down from your "freedom" high; be prepared for it, have a plan and support network nearby to be your mental aspirin for the ensuing "freedom high hangover". It may look like an "oh shit" moment where you question every decision you have made in your life up until that point and second guess getting out of the military. This is completely normal…I can say that because it happened to me every time I got out – and I turned out just fine (for the most part), just a few more bumps and bruises than I had expected.

Challenging Versus Difficult Versus Hard

This is my favorite example and approach to adopting a better/more successful perspective. I use it extensively in mentoring and coaching college students, active military, veterans, and even civilians who are changing careers.

Goals/situations/things are challenging, NOT difficult or hard; the perception of something being difficult acknowledges there is the possibility for failure; hard things include wood, metal, and concrete.

Acknowledging something is difficult is a conscious choice whereby you give yourself permission to fail. NOTE: you never fail as long as you learn from your mistakes – this ties directly back to Insanity.

To the best of my knowledge, a college homework

assignment or changing careers has never fallen from the sky and knocked anyone unconscious while they were walking down the sidewalk – therefore neither is "hard".

Success = Preparation + Opportunity (Bobby Unser; Zig Ziglar; Jimmy Johnson)

This is another great quote, and has been represented and attributed to at least a few different sources. It is a derivative from the quote from Senaca (circa 5 B.C.-65 A.D.), which stated "Luck is what happens when preparation meets opportunity". The modernized "success" versions/iterations/variants are an absolute/pinnacle/model for ensuring a successful military to civilian transition. It/they tells/remind us about every core military lesson/achievement…have a plan, and implement the plan at the most opportunistic time.

6 APTITUDE VERSUS PERCEPTION

Aptitude and Perception

Other's perceptions do not have to be your reality. This concept is a bit more blurred in the eyes of the civilian market. As military members, we have voluntarily chosen to serve our country and, if needed, are/were willing to make the ultimate sacrifice. Regardless of our rank, we all made the conscious choice to serve our nation; and we were all ultimately responsible to the mission, personnel, and equipment on our installations. With this understanding, rank then becomes a matter of accountability, level of functional practitioner proficiency, and pay scale.

Aptitude Translation

Translating your skills and accomplishments from military aptitude to civilian application can be a challenge. More than likely (regardless of rank), you were responsible (to varying degrees) for several to many hundreds of personnel (directly or indirectly); thousands to millions, perhaps even billions, of dollars of equipment; and ultimately to a cause/mission that few civilians would understand (acknowledge-yes, understand-more than likely not). Those who would most likely understand among civilian personnel include career fields such as law enforcement, fire-fighting/first responders, defense, national security, and other similar careers.

Aptitude Fallacy

I (as well as many other current/prior military members) have been told by potential employers that my military experience does not translate/equate/pertain/relate to XYZ/civilian job(s)… your experience absolutely does – DO NOT EVER BUY INTO THAT MENTALITY! The key is to translate your skills and experience into relevant and marketable civilian skills and terminology.

Aptitude - Example One

I recall after my third military to civilian transition, I had applied to a national retailer. I am not going to name the company specifically, but it is something you shoot at in the military during weapons qualification. By this time in my military career, I had accumulated six years active duty, 2.5 years in the reserves, and three years in the national guard – so approximately 11.5 years of service; 8.5 years of which I was a Security Police/Security Forces supervisor. When I had applied to the national retailer, I was told during the interview, the position required at least two years management/supervision experience and a four year college degree. I stated I had just completed my four-year degree a couple months prior, and that I had 8.5 years as a supervisor/manager with the military, plus an additional one year with state corrections for a total of 9.5 years of management/supervisory experience. The interviewer, a regional director, stated none of my management and supervision experience counted because it was military/government experience. I asked how my experience was different from what they were looking for? The interviewer replied "We are looking for someone with management skills, supervisory experience, and someone who has experience scheduling employees. Also, someone who understands budget, time off, disciplinary actions, award/recognition recommendations, individual and team development, policy compliance/enforcement, aspects of training, and who has had a fair amount of responsibility for merchandise/property." I replied, "I have been doing all of those things for over nine years." They stated, "Okay, but how many people have you supervised/reported on? This job requires you to be able to supervise two direct reports and a dozen indirect reports." I replied "I have had 4 to 22 direct reports; and indirectly in my direct reporting structure: up to 80 employees; indirectly, not in my direct reporting structure: up to 400 (working military, and inmates)." They said "Oh. Well, what is the dollar value of the inventory have you been responsible for? Our stores can contain several hundred thousand dollars of inventory, and we have hundreds of customers enter the store each day." I asked "Are we talking human capital or physical property? If we are talking human capital, I do not feel it fair to put a price tag on a person's life. In our capacity in the military (and state corrections for that matter), we are responsible for hundreds, and thousands, of peoples' lives daily. Our job is to protect not only the people in the military but to protect and serve our nation's peoples. If we are talking about physical property, I believe the dollar value of the military aircraft and the nuclear missiles I was responsible for were in the tens to hundreds of millions of dollars – each. I can offer additional clarification if you would like. I am also happy to answer any additional questions you may have. They said they did not have any additional questions and would get back to me. Even though the interviewer was a bit dismissive towards me, I remained respectful and kept my military bearing throughout the interview. Not to leave you hanging in suspense, I did end up getting the job. But it took work on my part to make the civilian regional director understand that my experience translated to and far exceeded their requirements. This job was a huge step down financially (minus 50%) for me from the military – even with a four-year college degree – but it was the first job that came my way after I got out of the military, so I took it.

Aptitude - Example Two

After about a year of retail management, and after completing my master's degree, I received a job offer from a defense contractor – this was about 2.5 years after my third military transition. By now I had 10.5

years of management experience and a master's degree. I had been applying for upper manager and director level positions in the defense contractor's security organization – both were positions I was VERY well qualified for. While I provided a convincing argument for my experience in the retail world, I was not as successful in the defense industry. They were firm and would not negotiate nor recognize/acknowledge my military experience as having any form of relevance. They stated, I only had 2.5 years of "real world" (in other words, a civilian) experience, and my military/government experience did not apply to their environment, and therefore I was not qualified for any security position except for entry level. Instead they offered me an entry level position in finance – because my master's degree was in business. I was still very qualified for several positions at higher levels in the company, my aptitude did not change, and the perception of the defense contractor did not either. However, after a couple years on the job, I did garner several advocates within the company and accumulated industry specific experience that complimented my transferable military skills, and took a positon in the operations organization. While I did not end up working directly for the security organization, I became an invaluable resource and business partner for them when the opportunity arose to help them revise and develop their policies and procedures – no one in my current organization had the experiential insight I had. The perception of my aptitude had changed significantly and I was perceived as a highly skilled resource. I know, this story did not end as cool as my last one with a "Hah! Take that to the bank!" Rather it provided the revelation that corporate America is VERY competitive, and organizations tend to promote from within…sounds a little like the military in some ways. The ultimate lesson was that I focused on my aptitude and positioned my experience/expertise within the needs of the company thereby altering their perception of my value. In other words, I adapted.

7 ADAPTING…

Adapting is About Attitude

Adapting is also conscious choice, and taking an attitudinal approach to overcoming obstacles and challenges. This exercise in becoming a civilian will test all aspects of your knowledge on adapting to new situations. There is a high probability you will question your decision to leave/retire from the military (as I did – three times). In the event it is NOT your choice to leave (like in the case of my third departure from the military, or retirement), you may find yourself questioning your skills, abilities, expertise, value, self-worth, etc. This too is normal. Take it in stride as a part of the "learning to adapt" process. You are a professional and an expert in every aspect, and your military training is proof.

Now is the time to test your training and skills in

adaption at the next level. Successful adaption will also depend on how proactively you have planned and prepared to make your transition, and your willingness to accept your new environments. Combining your skills and experience, reflecting on your military training, and taking a strategic and patient approach to adapting will help ensure you have covered most of the essential considerations.

Keep a Positive Attitude!

You have real value. Your training and security clearance (if you have one) is worth tens of thousands of dollars to potential employers. Additionally, the ability to quickly adapt to your surroundings, the team, management styles, adversity, and changing priorities sets you years ahead of your competition. You have plenty of value, so keep/maintain your positive outlook and attitude throughout this phase of the transition.

No is the answer. How many times have you been told "no" in the military? Guess what? It is going to happen in the civilian world too. Just like in the military, do not take it personally, remain professional, and hold your head high. You need to remember your value…as a professional, and monetarily from the investment in your military training. Statistically speaking, the more "no's" you receive, the more likely you are to receive a "yes" in the future.

Regarding our military bearing and professionalism…sometimes this can come across as aloof or distant (sometimes even a bit arrogant or cocky) – be professional but tempered, like when you attend a mandatory training; professional but a bit relaxed. The time and monetary investment the military made in you makes you a highly skilled professional and it commands a degree of acknowledgement in the civilian workplace; and a college degree in addition to your training will help to distinguish you among other applicants. Security clearances are another huge bonus to civilian employers. So, do not sell yourself short; you are a highly skilled professional, we just need to help you find a job/position/career you will be happy in and that is worthy of your skills.

Battle Scars, Bumps, and Bruises

Will you get through this relatively unscathed? – Yes, most likely, as long as you keep an open mind and are a WILLING PARTICIPANT in the transition process. As with many phases of the transition process, when you are adapting, you will find things that work well, and you will rejoice. You will also try things that do not work as well or simply do not work at all (not even remotely – just another FUBAR) – chalk these up to the learning and adaption process. Remember back to basic training…how many times did we incorrectly apply camouflage to our faces? (Sidebar: Really?...Is there a way to incorrectly apply camouflage paint to our faces? You put various non-human colors on your face so it does not look like a face anymore – easy-peezy. Though, I do recall one buddy in training applying camouflage paint to his field buddy. Technically he did a good job. However, the instructor failed to find the humor in the black on green peace symbol on his buddy's face.) When we try something that does not end in desirable results, learn from the positive and negative aspects of that approach. Repeat the positive processes, discard the negative practices. As long as you are learning and not repeating mistakes, you are succeeding.

8 ...AND OVERCOMING

The sheer power and will of a team cannot be underestimated or undervalued. Overcoming is about networking and support; it truly takes a team. Do not try to be a hero and grind through this process on your own – the battle scars are not worth it. Remember, this is coming from a three-time world champ of trying to transition on his own.

Two of your greatest assets as a current/former military member are your abilities to adapt and work in teams. This will be immediately tested from day one. First, you will need to start adapting to being a civilian from the onset...but what does that mean? To start with it means you should seek out a colleague, mentor, coach, friend, relative, or professional transition expert (in other words, a team member) to help you with the transition. Second, expand your professional network. Third, build several different resumes (this is tedious and time consuming but will pay dividends when applying for jobs – more on this later). Finally, lean/depend on your support network (personal and professional). This may feel awkward or counter-intuitive because as team members, we are trained to check our emotions at the door. However, this will reduce your levels of stress and frustration in the long run. Transitioning is not an individual sporting event or activity. Successful transitioning is about putting together a good team. Do we enter a hostile or unknown combative situation alone? – No. The same holds true for transitioning to civilian status. It takes a team!

DR. DAVID P. PELTZ

9 STRESS VERSUS FRUSTRATION

There is a Difference – Know It

While working at the state prison as a corrections officer, I learned the beginning of a powerful lesson. I was having a bad day, and an inmate said to me "Hey, CO, you look like you are having a bad day." I said "Yup, we all do from time to time." He said "Hey, man, don't sweat the small shit, you get go home every night." It helped me to realize there is a very powerful and marked distinction between stress and frustration. Fundamentally speaking, people deal differently with stress versus frustration. The key thing here is to recognize and understand the difference between the two. From a military perspective, we are trained how to manage and control ourselves in stressful environments/situations. Below are operational definitions of stress and frustration.

Stress is a cognitive response. Our jobs in a corporate or non-life threatening environments are not stressful however, they can be challenging and frustrating (recognize the difference). Having a job or work that is stressful includes those where there is immediate threat/risk to life (yours or others) such as first responders, firefighters, law enforcement, medical emergency/surgical, and military.

Frustration is an emotional response borne from the lack of capacity, functional position, authority to influence others or the situation to achieve a desired outcome. Simply stated, it is essentially the challenges we encounter with inter and/or intra organizational cultures, climates, personal and professional interactions, and decision making.

Acknowledge and Accept the Difference

Acknowledging the difference between stress and frustration will help you, and others, correctly respond to situations. In the military, we understand stress. We understand what it is and how to effectively engage and overcome most stressful situations. Most civilians (except for the career fields mentioned above), on the other hand, do not know what it is like to work in a truly stressful environment. Their misperception of stress is further propagated through others who do not truly understand stress, thereby creating a misguided work environment focused on "deadlines" as the cause of stress. In reality, most "deadlines" are really "due dates", which are primarily affected by proper or improper planning and execution of those plans.

Instances of confusion. Several, and often, times in the civilian business environment, I have encountered "stressed out" coworkers. When I asked them about the situation, the conversation would always go something to the effect of them saying "I/we are not going to meet the deadline for XYZ project! We are so screwed!" Their perception of the situation was that it was perhaps more dire than it really was. I would follow up with "Why are we screwed? What is going to happen if we do not finish the project on time?" They would look at me like I was an idiot and say "If we do not meet the deadline for the project it will delay the release date/start of production! Then the manager/director/vice president/president/CEO will want to know why. There is the very real possibility we could lose our jobs or face disciplinary action!" I would reply calmly "So, no one is going to get hurt or die, and no one's life is in danger, correct?" Again, looking at me like I had no clue, they would say "What? What does that have to do with anything? No…no, no one will get hurt or die!" From which I would reply "So everyone is safe? Everyone gets to go home tonight? What is the problem? So what if things are delayed a day/week/month/cancelled? So what if we lose our jobs? At least we are all safe from harm and can come back tomorrow and figure out a viable solution." I would tell them "Stress is a reaction; frustration is an emotion. Stress evokes a fight or flight mechanism inside of us; frustration is an emotional response to something we dislike." The looks on their faces is always priceless. What they were experiencing was not stress but rather frustration. Inevitably, their blood pressure would drop, they would start breathing normally, and a normal color would return to their faces. Because I had remained calm and aware, they too became calm and aware. Now, if they would have come to me saying there was a pack of wild rabid bears or lions running around the office eating people – I would admittedly concur that we were officially engaged in a stressful situation.

Conscious Reminders

Reminding ourselves and others about the real difference between stress and frustration enables us to step back and assess the situation for what it is. It allows us to become more conscious of our surroundings and facilitates a more rational work environment based upon awareness. If we are not going to make a due date for a project, we need to understand what lead to that outcome, develop a plan to ensure the situation will not repeat itself, and communicate our finding/the situation with the responsible parties involved.

10 RESPONSIBILITY

Understanding Responsibility

True depth of responsibility. While serving in the military, we learn to define responsibility based upon the physical property and human capital within our scope of impact. Physical property can include structures/facilities, munitions, weapon systems, installations, air/ground/water craft/transportation, food stores, IT/computer systems, and administrative supplies, just to name a few. It may also include various aspects of intellectual property. The total property we are accountable for can range from the thousands to hundreds of millions of dollars, sometimes even more. Human capital refers to individuals within our chain of command, and those that we are directly and indirectly accountable to, based upon our assigned/chosen career field. The human capital aspect cannot be, in all fairness, monetized – nor should it. We all understand the oath we took whereby we agreed to sacrifice our own lives for the betterment our nation – unfortunately, some of our colleagues, friends, and family have made this sacrifice.

Translating Responsibility

Making responsibility understandable to others. In the civilian world, it can be challenging to translate our level of military responsibility into something similar in the civilian environment. I encountered this while working in retail management. The store inventory was valued in the millions of dollars, and the department managers and store manager were often boastful of how much inventory they controlled and maintained. Often times I found it challenging to translate the value of being a Security Forces supervisor/manager. I was responsible for properly deploying several armed Security Forces members in a first responder capacity in the event of an emergency that could involve military and civilian people. The dollar value within my scope of responsibility surpassed the value of all the clothing, lawn, music, game, computer, and food items in the whole store. My job in the military, could easily be translated to civilian "law enforcement". However, not many civilian law enforcement member patrol daily with an arsenal of automatic weapons in armored vehicles...with several other team equally equipped (along with other "tools" of the trade). Another example, one of my best friends was a cook in the military...how does that translate? I could say he was a chef or caterer but neither of those terms really does justice for someone who was responsible for providing food preparation and meals for thousands of personnel...three times a day...every day of the week/365, in addition to the fiduciary, financial, and logistical responsibilities.

How could I/we possibly convey the scope and level of responsibility that we had in the military and correlate it to being a retail manager, or college recruiter, or any other non-military job for that matter? We can identify the transferable skills we possess by breaking down what we do/did in the military to its core skills. Those common core skills become our focus, and are referred to as transferable skills. Focusing on the transferable skills attempts, and usually does, level set the field from a practical job perspective. When done properly, it typically displays how highly qualified we are, on many levels.

Human Capital of Responsibility

People as facets of responsibly. In the military, we are accustomed to operating within a budget. We know how many heads we have/need to maintain our working schedules, and maintain our tools and equipment. When someone moves on to another installation, somcone else replaces them. When an item breaks down, we fix it or replace it. To us, it is all about getting the job done. In the civilian world, the same can be said with one MAJOR exception...the constant consideration of the bottom line profits and cost expenditures. In the military, more times than not, we are not overly concerned with the "profitability" of our job (i.e., how much money we are making for the government/military). Rather, our primary focus is doing our job well and keeping the country and our allies safe from harm. While safety is a valid concern for civilian companies, how much money the company is making is the main reason they are in business. Profitability is king, and resources and consumables are judiciously utilized to maximize profit and reduce expenses. It is not uncommon for companies in some industries to conduct one or more internal reorganizations/restructurings each year to boost their profitability. The inevitable result of these reorganizations/restructurings is that typically one to many employees are let go or laid off. While this looks good on paper for the profitability of the company, it can and typically does have a major negative impact on morale. The reason for addressing this topic is to help you realize the potential cost of doing business in a civilian environment. In the military, we do not worry about job security and being "let go" (until our contract is up). The other reason is, for some of us, we may be hired into a job requiring us to not only make recommendations for promotion/disciplinary action, but also hired for being THAT person to do the hiring/firing/letting go of employees. It is another level/degree to our responsibility that we may or may not be used to accomplishing as a normal part of our jobs.

Satisfaction of Responsibility

Find and/or redefine your purpose. In light of your new-found circumstances (transitioning military), you may need to periodically redefine what responsibility means to you; this may include finding a new and/or different purpose. Traditionally, responsibility to those of us in the military may carry significantly different undertones than to our civilian counterparts. Meaning, even though our military jobs may appear very similar or potentially identical to some civilian jobs, there is the facet of national security and service to our country that may not necessarily apply to the civilian position. This factor places what we do/did in the military in a slightly different category of being responsible. This is further compounded if we are assigned to an overseas installation or in a hostile/war time/combat situation. Fundamentally speaking, translating this level of responsibly to an apparently identical civilian job can be challenging at best. While some employers state that they understand our level of responsibility (potentially from a functional perspective), they may not realize that for us, just doing our job may not provide the same degree of satisfaction for us as did the same job in the military. This is directly due to the gap in responsibility – and is something we must accept and own.

Satisfaction of responsibility tested. As a part of my Air Force/military career, I had the opportunity to work on a counter drug task force in the National Guard. It was a joint Army and Air Guard task force, whereby I trained with and was certified as a U.S. Army Instructor. I used my instructor certification on the task force, and also created intergraded Army and Air Guard law enforcement training. I put my trainer skills to work while employed with the defense contractor as well. The attitude towards the training development, delivery, and the course content was…different. While the course content was safety compliance related, and could ultimately affect human life, there was a rather lax attitude towards us as trainers. It was as if what we were creating was somewhat of a nuisance for employees when they had to complete the training we created. Feeling empowered, respected, and important, we did not. I say 'we' because there were only a few veterans on the team. Yet in the military, if you are/were an instructor, it was saying (in many cases) you were an expert in the content and delivery of that content. It was a respectful position to have. As a result, this perception affected our feeling of satisfaction towards developing training. In the military, what we did was appreciated. But, that was not the case with this defense contractor. Conversely, when I worked in the technology sector, trainers were respected and appreciated, though significantly overworked.

Leadership of Responsibility

Leading in your job. Many civilians view their jobs just simply as jobs – work to be done. Others perceive their job as the source of importance, value and/or symbol of positional responsibility/power in comparison to others. This perception of positional responsibility and authority (while warranted in some cases), in many cases, was strictly position based. To delineate further, it has been my experience and observation, that many civilian positions of authority/responsibility are filled with technical experts who have little to no real management and/or leadership experience. The clearest example of this I can provide was when I worked for the defense contractor. I spoke with a newly promoted upper manager who was a little full of themselves, attitudinally speaking. The manager told me that he really did not want the job but took it for two reasons: because their director valued them as an expert engineer, and for the hefty pay raise. I asked them how they felt about being a manger and leader. They replied, "Anyone can be a manager". I asked them how they felt about being a leader. They said, "Anyone can be a leader/manager because it was all the same stuff." I replied, "So, if you are an expert engineer you are an expert as a manager/leader as well." They replied, "Pretty much, yes." I followed this up with "I am an expert in leadership too, I have a PhD in leadership. Would you agree I too am an expert leader?". They replied, "Absolutely, you are a doctor." I replied, "Since I work closely as engineering support staff, can I help with engineering the missile?" The manager's eyes went wide open and they said "No, absolutely not! You are not an engineer; you need an engineering degree, highly specialized training, and years of experience to be an engineer!" I replied, "My point exactly. Just because you are an expert engineer does not make you an expert in leadership without years of training, education and experience." This manager conceded to my point and acknowledged that the field of leadership was not an area he possessed any level of expertise in. So, when we find/redefine our purpose we also need to redefine our understanding of responsibility from a leadership/self-leadership perspective. We need to always keep in mind our leadership training as a facet of responsibility. A few people you will encounter will get the "it" about what it means to serve our country and be a leader in the military. Many people who have not been in the military will never get the "it" piece however, they will appreciate our service – it is up to us to help those people understand our value as military leaders.

DR. DAVID P. PELTZ

PART III: TACTICAL ELEMENTS AND TOOLS

11. Need for Higher Education
    i.   Degree Progression History
    ii. The Reality of College Education.
    iii. Institution Types
    iv. College Modalities
    v.   National versus Regional Accreditation
    vi. Perceptions of University Types
    vii. Final Thought

12. Types of Certifications and Licenses

13. Job Search Web Sites

14. Recruiting/Headhunter Agencies, and Internal Recruiters Versus Job Service Agencies
    i.   Recruiting/Headhunters Agencies
    ii. Internal Company Recruiters
    iii. Job Service Agencies
    iv. Read Your Contract!

15. Resumes for Your Toolbox
    i.   Government Resume
    ii. Detailed Resume
    iii. Professional Resume
    iv. Targeted Resume
    v.   Chronological Resume
    vi. Skill Based Resume
    vii. Cover Letters

11 NEED FOR HIGHER EDUCATION

This is perhaps the most important section in this part of the book. It can potentially save you from making a mistake costing you tens of thousands of dollars, several years of coursework, and ultimately attending non-transferable college classes.

Degree Progression History

The need for higher learning has been around for several decades. Over the past century, marked intervals have shown attaining a degree in higher education is important for distinguishing one candidate above another. As a result, higher education credentials can represent a powerful competitive edge in the job market. In the early 1900's through about the early 1960's, having a high school diploma set you apart from most others, when it comes to education.

In the mid-1960' through mid-1980's, and Associate's degree would set you apart from the majority of your peers. In the late 1980's through about 2000, a Bachelor's/undergraduate degree would serve as point of distinction. By the turn of the 21st century, approximately 38% of the U.S. population had an undergraduate degree. Hence, from about 2000 on, a Master's/graduate degree has become the new standard to distinguish one candidate above another as competition differentiator. At the time of this writing, approximately 18% of the U.S. population have a graduate degree. Doctorate degrees (of just about any sort) provide an additional level of prestige since this achievement is only represented by approximately 4% of the U.S. population. Therefore, over the past 100 years, completing a college degree at the minimum, has become increasingly important to secure a solid position in the job market. Gone, for over a decade, are the days where experience alone will get you a good paying job (with very few exceptions).

The Reality of College Education

A college degree is no longer an option; it is a requirement. Having a high school diploma, or a high school diploma and Associates degree are not enough to be truly competitive when trying to secure a decent paying job with a good company. While the Associate's degree is a good stepping stone in your military career, in the long run it can take one to two years longer to complete your Bachelor's/undergraduate degree. If you can get an Associate's degree along the way to your Bachelor's degree, great! If not, I would not sweat it, personally (and professionally) speaking. Once you have achieved a Bachelor's degree, an Associate's degree appears as a 'minor' to your Bachelor's degree because all Associate's level courses are typically in the lower division level at the 100-200 level coursework; whereas your major takes place in the upper division 300-400 level courses.

Experience Alone is not Enough

Gone are the days when simply having 5, 10, 15, 20 or even 30 years of job/professional experience will get you a good paying job. While these years of experience and expertise bode well in the military; in the civilian sector, experience alone is just not enough. As a general rule, many companies, corporations, government agencies, educational institutions, and businesses now require a Bachelor's degree as a minimum requirement to get into salaried position.

Being Competitive in the Job Market

To be competitive in the job market, you will need a college degree (undergraduate or higher). The more education the better, especially when it is being paid for by the U.S. military. Gone too are the days where employers promote/reward you for getting a college degree; and gone are the days where employers pay for all/most of your college education (with limited exceptions). Some employers will still pay for your college degree but either at a reduced annual rate that will equate to about half the courses taken during the school year, and/or will require you to stay employed with them for a few years after you have finished your degree. If you leave prior to the required "sticking around" time, you face paying back all or part of the tuition assistance they have provided to you attended school under their employment. Each company has its own rules, so ensure you are VERY familiar with education programs and reimbursement policies and criteria.

Time Versus Money

Time versus money facet of education. Time versus money is a very real phenomenon when getting your education. Only taking the number of courses an employer will cover each year may seem like a great way to get your college degree paid for (if your employer offers education assistance). The catch here is two-fold. Firstly, time is money. Instead of completing a Master's degree in say two years going full time (in addition to working full time – this is possible, thousands of working adults do this each year), it may take the better part of four to four and half years. That is two to two and half years of lost potential earned income at a higher rate of pay.

Additionally, many undergraduate and graduate programs are offered with a set course sequence. Schools are intentionally designing degree programs to have the most current and relevant content and information. If the course sequence is not followed in the designated order, you may experience a delay in resuming your program. Delays can equate to several months, or in some cases even a year or more. Not only will this take you even longer to complete your degree, you may miss the time constraints for finishing your degree, and consequently lose some or all your college degree progress. The sooner you can complete your college degree, the sooner you can be more competitive for jobs and or promotions.

Closer to a Degree Than You May Realize

With your military trainings (some of which convert to college credits), most enlisted military members are only about two years (sometimes a little less) away from completing their Bachelor's degree. This is an incentive to complete your college degree, and the sooner the better. Use the military training that equates to college credits to your advantage.

Education Versus Income Versus Opportunity

There is a known model of education versus opportunity versus income. As one increases their level of education so does too their opportunity to earn more annual income. Along with that it shows that as one increases their level of education, there are fewer jobs that require such higher level of education. It displays that those with a high school diploma have a reasonable range of job opportunities, but at a very low income level. Those individuals with an undergraduate degree have access to additional job opportunities, and income opportunity is doubled. Those individuals with a graduate/Master's degree have less job opportunities proportionately than those with a Bachelor's/undergraduate degree, yet their income opportunity can easily be 50% to 75% higher than those with a just Bachelor's degree. Those who have earned a Doctorate degree have a relatively small niche of job options (because they have specialized in a specific area) however, their income potential is significantly higher than those with a Master's degree; whereby "significantly" can easily equate to 50% or double, triple or even more. This is easy to observe in the military ranking structure where there are greater numbers of lower ranking persons in the military performing task based work in comparison with higher ranking persons in management and leadership roles. Similarly, corporate work structures also typically have more line staff than leadership roles.

Institution Types

Public/State Versus Private

There are a couple of basic categories of higher education institutions: public/state and private. Private institutions are privately held/owned business entities; and public/state/community institutions are held by the state/community/county/city. There are pros and cons to each. Some private institutions can cost two to three times more than their public/state counterparts. However, over the past decade or so, most state university tuitions are catching up with the cost of private institution tuitions (not including the elite ivy league universities like Yale and Harvard, to name a few).

Secular Versus Religious Affiliated

Attending secular/traditional schools versus faith-based/religious affiliated schools is a matter of personal preference. My first two degrees (undergraduate/Bachelor's and graduate/Master's) were from a private for-profit university. I received a good solid education and have no complaints. I completed my Doctorate degree from a faith-based/religious affiliated university and viewed it as an opportunity to expand my knowledge. I viewed it as receiving a minor in theological business leadership applications. Attending a state university, one may have to pay for this minor separately, mine was integrated into my doctoral education. Some business entities appreciate the faith-based/religious affiliated integration as it can tend to produce more ethical graduates. For example, the university I earned my Doctorate degree from was regularly solicited by the U.S. government for its law students.

For-Profit Versus Non-Profit Versus Not-For-Profit

Colleges and universities are also divided by their income/revenue categories. Just like any other business, they can fall in to for-profit, non-profit, and not-for-profit. Each business type has its company tax and income recognition advantages/disadvantages depending upon the goal of the institution. Virtually all state-run schools fall into the non-profit category. Many private run colleges and universities are for-profit but not all, some are non-profit. Most faith-based or religiously affiliated schools are non-profit or not-for-profit, although there are some that are for-profit. Their financial category tends to affect their tuition costs, overall student body size, and physical footprint. Quality of education will be discussed in the section on accreditation.

College Modalities

Up through the mid 1970's, there was only one real modality for going to college – you went to college – that is, you went into a physical classroom and sat down in a chair to attend class. Currently, there are three basic college modalities: traditional (as just described), online, and blended (as implied, it is a blending of traditional and online). Most/virtually all state higher education institutions have an online learning component/modality. Traditional attendance can be defined by physical class attendance one or more days per week. Online attendance is typically defined by the number of days (and responses) a student participates in the virtual discussion threads that take place between instructor and other students. Blended attendance is typically a combination of limited physical attendance combined with more online attendance/presence. Each has its pros and cons. Traditional schooling is great for networking, getting to know other students and the instructor, immediate responses and organic discussions, and instant feedback/clarification however, you must be available to physically attend class throughout the week(ends) during the day and/or evenings. Online allows for much more flexibility in one's schedule however, there is a greater degree of learner autonomy. The technology facet (internet connection, email, discussion forum posting, etc.) can potentially result in a higher performance/participation expectation. Blended allows the best of both worlds, if that is what you are seeking – in person relationships and instructor guidance combined with the classroom flexibility, and learning from just about anywhere.

National Versus Regional Accreditation

ACCREDITATION IS THE MOST IMPORTANT FACTOR IN SELECTING YOUR COLLEGE EDUCATION. Not all schools are created equal. There are two primary types of accreditation: national and regional. One IS better than the other – do not be fooled. The best analogy I can provide is that national accreditation is like the federal law, everyone must abide by it; regional accreditation is like state law, the states can make the laws tougher than the federal law but not more lenient. Therefore, **regional accreditation is more desirable/better – as they are held to higher educational standards from the Higher Learning Commission (HLC)**.

I have talked to many dozens of students who have attended colleges/universities that were/are nationally accredited only for them to find out that their 3.5 years of college did not transfer to a state or private regionally accredited college/university. Yes, they essentially lost one to three years of college courses (and the money they paid/invested in tuition costs/fees). Virtually all regionally accredited colleges have stopped accepting college credits from nationally accredited institutions.

Regional accreditation governing bodies include the following:

1. MSA (Middle States Association of Colleges and Schools)
2. NEASC (New England Association of Schools and Colleges)
3. NCA (North Central Association of Colleges and Schools)
4. NAC (Northwest Accreditation Commission)
5. SACS (Southern Association of Colleges and Schools)
6. WASC (Western Association of Schools and Colleges)

(www.geteducated.com/regional-vs-national-accreditation-which-is-better-for-online-colleges)
(www.guidetoonlineschools.com/resources/accreditation/regional-accreditation?page=)

All regionally accredited colleges and universities will indicate somewhere on their web site they are regionally accredited. This can be typically located under About or Accreditation, or by typing in "accreditation" in the search block. In some cases, it may be easier to call or email them to find the accreditation level.

Perceptions of University Types

Over the past 45 years, the perceptions and attitudes towards getting a college degree from a traditional versus online university have changed. Initially, from the mid-1970's through the very early 2000's, people and companies questioned the quality of education from an online institution. Beginning in the early 2000's (around the 2005 period), state colleges and ivy league universities started adding online degree programs as a modality option. Now prestigious institutions, such as Harvard, have online degree programs. You may hear how this college or that college has had accreditation issues in the past, and that may well be true, but that does not make one necessarily better or worse than another. Even state universities have occasional brushes with losing accreditation or have lost accreditation.

Final Thought

If you take nothing else away from this discussion on getting/completing a four-year college degree REMEMBER TO ATTEND A COLLEGE/UNIVERSITY THAT IS REGIONALLY ACCREDITED.

12 TYPES OF CERTIFICATIONS AND LICENSES

There are several professional certifications available. You may be familiar with or have heard about some of them. These professional certifications/licenses will add to your credentialing, depending on the field/industry you work in. You may already have one or more of these depending upon your own personal/professional development in the military. Most (if not all) of these certifications typically cost several thousands of dollars (unless sponsored/conducted by your employer); and some require formal membership and certification renewal fees. Some of the licenses are issued by each individual state, so be sure to familiarize yourself with the state/local licensing requirements for the area/state you desire to license in. This is a sample list and will provide a general high level overview on some of the certifications and licenses available. It may also provide you with some options to consider and explore. Below are very brief generalized descriptions of 22 certifications and licenses. When these licenses are combined with a Bachelor's degree or higher, the employee value increases significantly.

Six Sigma

A Six Sigma certification is focused on quality and statistical analysis. The Six Sigma standards were originally branded by Motorola [and popularized by Jack Welsh at General Electric]. The primary recognized source for Six Sigma certifications is the American Society for Quality or ASQ. Several schools and colleges offer coursework for preparation for this certification. Additionally, several companies now offer their own flavor of internal Six Sigma certifications. The distinctions between in-house Six Sigma certifications are the associated rigor and overall industry acceptance of the certification. An analogy (in car/vehicle terms): it is the difference between a Cadillac and a Chevrolet; a Lexus and a Toyota; a Lincoln and a Ford; an Infinity and a Nissan; an Acura and a Honda. While they are very similar, the overall quality and acceptance industry version from ASQ is superior to an in-house version. That being said, having an in-house Six Sigma certification is definitely better than not having one.
asq.org/

Lean

Lean certifications are based in the field of process improvement. The primary focus is on the reduction of seven forms of waste (e.g., time, overproduction, rework, inventory, etc.). The primary recognized source for Lean certifications is also through ASQ. Several companies now offer their own flavor of internal Lean certifications. The distinctions between in-house Lean certifications are the associated rigor and overall acceptance of the certification. An analogy (in car/vehicle terms): it is the difference between a Cadillac and a Chevrolet; a Lexus and a Toyota; a Lincoln and a Ford; an Infinity and a Nissan; an Acura and a Honda. While they are very similar, the overall quality and acceptance industry version from ASQ is superior to an in-house version. That being said, having an in-house Lean certification is definitely better than not having one.

asq.org/

Lean/Six Sigma

Just as the certification title implies, it is a combined certification between Lean and Six Sigma. This can be a time consuming, yet valuable certification. It blends the concepts and tools of the two certifications into one or more certification(s). While Lean and Six Sigma work well together, they are vastly different. Hence, achieving this certification combines the best of both worlds but, as mentioned, it may take a bit more time to complete because of the dual nature of the certification.

www.iassc.org/

Lean Startup

While not as formal a certification as the other Lean areas, it does offer several valuable training options in the area of Lean Startup. Eric Reis (2011) is the primary authority in Lean Startup. It is based on five guiding principles whereby developing "a minimum viable product" is at its crux. Development of the minimum viable product/service provides a basis for moving forward with that offering at the earliest viable moment in the offering's development. It is very useful for those seeking to become entrepreneurs or are engaged in internal company startup project products and services.

theleanstartup.com/

Agile

IC Agile is the official source and offers several certifications and classes. IC Agile clearly states Agile is not a methodology but rather an "approach". One of the primary philosophies is Scrum. Scrum is based in constant consistent ongoing feedback for project performance and process improvements. It is currently the basis of understanding and application development in many companies in the technology sector.

icagile.com

Project Management Professional (PMP)

The Project Management Institute (PMI) is the premier institute for this type of industry certification. PMI offers several valuable certifications in the areas of project and program management, and is perhaps the most widely recognized entity for these types of certifications. As the name implies, the Project Management Professional certification revolves around project management and related techniques and principles. Several schools and colleges offer coursework for preparation for this certification. Additionally, several companies now offer their own flavor of internal Project Management certifications. The distinctions between in-house Project Management certifications are the associated rigor and overall acceptance of the certification. An analogy (in car/vehicle terms): it is the difference between a Cadillac and a Chevrolet; a Lexus and a Toyota; a Lincoln and a Ford; an Infinity and a Nissan; an Acura and a Honda. While they are very similar, the overall quality and acceptance industry version from PMI is superior to an in-house version. That being said, having an in-house Project Management certification is definitely better than not having one.

www.pmi.org/

Program Management Professional (PgMP)

The Project Management Institute (PMI) is the premier institute for this type of industry certification. PMI offers several valuable certifications in the areas of project and program management, and is perhaps the most widely recognized entity for these types of certifications. As the name implies, the Program Management Professional certification revolves around program management and related techniques and principles. Several schools and colleges offer coursework for preparation for this certification. Additionally, several companies now offer their own flavor of internal Program Management certifications. The distinctions between in-house Program Management certifications are the associated rigor and overall acceptance of the certification. An analogy (in car/vehicle terms): it is the difference between a Cadillac and a Chevrolet; a Lexus and a Toyota; a Lincoln and a Ford; an Infinity and a Nissan; an Acura and a Honda. While they are very similar, the overall quality and acceptance industry version from PMI is superior to an in-house version. That being said, having an in-house Program Management certification is definitely better than not having one. www.pmi.org/

Certified Public Accountant (CPA)

Each state has their own individual board certified licensing requirements. This licensure requires a combination of experience and education requirements. Usually a four-year college degree in accounting is required. Some states may require a few additional college courses to meet the basic education requirements. A graduate/Master's degree in this field usually provides candidates with the proper education preparation for the state required exams. Once the education requirement is met, there is usually an experience requirement that follows, whereby the candidate for this certification works under the guidance of a currently licensed CPA for a specified period of time before they can sit for the state licensing exam. If interested in this license, ensure to familiarize yourself with your state's requirements, as they may vary slightly among states.

Professional in Human Resources (PHR-various)

The Professional in Human Resources certification is for people/professionals in the field of human resources. This entity provides a certification that is a bit more technically oriented than others. It is also widely accepted and respected.
www.hrci.org/

SHRM Certified Professional (SHRM-SCP-various)

The Society for Human Resources Management (SHRM) Certified Professional is for people/professionals in the field of human resources. This entity provides a certification that is a bit more experientially oriented than others. It too is widely accepted and respected.
www.shrm.org/

Licensed Practical Nurse (LPN)

This is an entry level nursing certification/licensure that can be attained after one to two years of schooling in the specified program. It provides general working knowledge of the nursing career. It is NOT a prerequisite for becoming a Registered Nurse.

Registered Nurse (RN)

A Registered Nurse is a state licensed nursing professional. Typically, this is a four-year college degree program. For the past couple of decades there has been a shortage of nurses in the field, so a great opportunity exists for this type of work. There are still some two-year college degree programs available that will provide the necessary coursework and training to sit for the state board (each state has their own requirements). The caveat to a two-year program is the two-year program usually takes three to four years to complete, and you end up with only an Associate's degree. In relatively the same amount of time it would take you to get an Associate's degree in nursing, you can complete a Bachelor's degree in nursing. A Bachelor's degree in nursing will provide more opportunity for career advancement in the future.

Real-estate

Since the housing market crash in 2008, and over the past several years, the real-estate market has been making a gradual come back. This is being made possible through record low interest rates, and increased lender accountability, whereby lending institutions are required to take on less mortgage lending risk. Depending on the local housing market, this state issued license can offer a good supplement/part-time income, or even a full-time income source. Each state has their own requirements, and there are typically a couple of local real-estate preparation training schools in most larger cities (and of course online).

Certified Professional Property Manager (CPP-various) (DOD property)

This certification is for people/professionals in the

field of logistics and government property management. It focusses on the tactical facets of the field as applied to government owned property. Those in the field of logistics and/or supply chain may benefit from this certification.

www.npma.org

Industrial Contract Property Management (ICPM-various) (DAWIA)

This certification is for people/professionals in the field of logistics and government property management and is offered by the Defense Acquisition University (DAU). It is a well-respected certification in the defense industry for those individuals involved with property management. It focusses a bit more on the contractual requirements of government property management as applied to government owned property. Those in the field of logistics and/or supply chain may benefit from this certification.

www.dau.mil/

Business Intelligence

This certification is typically offered at the undergraduate or graduate level. Several institutions offer this certification in traditional and online modalities. Its primary focus is in the areas of business analysis and decision performance and optimization. A general search of the internet will yield several degree and institution options to explore.

Business Analytics

This certification is typically offered at the undergraduate or graduate level. Several institutions offer this certification in traditional and online modalities. Its primary focus is in the areas of statistical analysis and metrics building and development for departments and organizations at a technical level. A general search of the internet will yield several degree and institution options to explore.

Data Analytics

This certification is typically offered at the undergraduate or graduate level. Several institutions offer this certification in traditional and online modalities. Its primary focus is in the areas of statistical analysis and data analysis for departments and organizations at a technical level. A general search of the internet will yield several degree and institution options to explore.

Data Science

This certification is typically offered at the undergraduate or graduate level. Several institutions offer this certification in traditional and online modalities. Its primary focus is in the areas of statistical analysis and metrics building for departments and organizations at a strategic level. A general search of the internet will yield several degree and institution options to explore.

Cisco (various)

This certification is typically offered at the undergraduate or graduate level. Several institutions offer this certification in traditional and online modalities. Its primary focus is in the areas of IT networking and platform development for departments and organizations at a technical level. This certification pairs very well with an undergraduate or graduate level technology degree.

Citrix (various)

This certification is typically offered at the undergraduate or graduate level. Several institutions offer this certification in traditional and online modalities. Its primary focus is in the areas of IT app/application and data delivery development for departments and organizations at a technical level. This certification pairs very well with an undergraduate or graduate level technology degree.

Information Security (IS)/Information Systems Security (ISS), (various)

These certifications are typically offered at the undergraduate or graduate level. Several institutions offer these certifications in traditional and online modalities. Their primary focus is in the areas of IT security/secure networking and systems platform development for departments and organizations at a technical level. This certification pairs very well with an undergraduate or graduate level technology degree.

13 JOB SEARCH WEB SITES

There are several job search sites available on the internet. Most provide a free basic limited service and typically offer a few paid premium service options (some are worth the extra cost for their premium services). Each of these tools will require a separate individual profile to be developed. I always encourage people to capture all their relevant professional information and education in a separate document, then copy and paste as needed to reduce manually recreating each profile. The information contained in the 11 descriptions below regarding the quality about each job search site is my own view based upon my personal experiences with each site.

LinkedIn (national and international-all regions)

Excellent for networking and job seekers. Many professionals have robust profiles on LinkeIn as it increases their professional networking visibility. Many employers also review the LinkedIn profiles of potential job candidates to learn more about a person's professional background and education.
www.linkedin.com/

Glassdoor

Great for finding job postings, company reviews, and company functional position salary information. The company reviews can help you decide if this company is a good fit for you. The functional salary information will help you to determine what your salary package should look like within a given company or industry. You may be surprised to find out you may be expecting too much or too little based upon your experience and education. This site's information is good to combine/compare with Indeed.
www.glassdoor.com/index.htm

Indeed

Great for finding job postings, company reviews, and company functional position salary information. The company reviews can help you decide if this is a company you want to work for. The functional salary information will help you to determine what your salary package should look like within a given company or industry. You may be surprised to find out you may be expecting too much or too little based upon your experience and education. This site's

information is good to combine/compare with Glassdoor.
www.indeed.com/

HigerEdJobs (national and international-all regions)

Great for finding teaching, faculty, staff, administration positions in higher education. It also provides opportunities offered outside of the U.S.
www.higheredjobs.com/

USAJobs (national and international-all regions)

Great for government entity job listings. Recently, the site has been overhauled and is more user friendly. While a government resume is highly recommended (all your normal resume information plus more detail and the kitchen sink and tires from your car), it is not necessarily required. The site is much easier to navigate and use however, you are still working with government agencies so response times…can……be……...rather……….slow.
www.usajobs.gov/

Virtual Vocations

Great for finding virtual/remote jobs. Many companies and industries are finding value in hiring individuals outside the local commuting area. This site provides a variety of positions across several industries across the U.S. Remote/virtual jobs allow you to work from home. Some companies may require you to physically be in the office a couple times per week, or a week a month, or a week a quarter, etc., or not at all depending on the job requirements and what was negotiated.

www.virtualvocations.com/

Bayt (international-Gulf/Middle East regions)

Good for finding job postings in the Middle East and Gulf regions. Dubai still remains a solid international job option when compared to some other country job markets.

www.bayt.com/

TheLadders

In the early 2000's this was a good site. It seems to provide somewhat higher level paying opportunities and may not be as robust as some of the other sites. I have found most opportunities listed here also appear on LinkedIn, Indeed, and Glassdoor.

www.theladders.com/

CareerBuilder

In the early 2000's this was a good site. It seems to provide somewhat lower level paying local opportunities and may not be as robust as some of the other sites. I have found most opportunities listed here also appear on LinkedIn, Indeed, and Glassdoor.

www.careerbuilder.com/

Monster

In the early 2000's this was a good site. It seems to

provide somewhat lower level paying local opportunities and may not be as robust as some of the other sites. I have found most opportunities listed here also appear on LinkedIn, Indeed, and Glassdoor.

www.monster.com/

Company Specific Sites

Individual company specific web sites will always provide a better job search option. The challenge is to be familiar enough with your industry section to know what other companies exist within that industry. Additionally, often small and mid-sized companies do not advertise their jobs on large internet job posting sites. Also, be willing to use/apply your skills in other industries where your skill set can be transferred. You may be surprised at the options that may exist.

14 RECRUITING/HEADHUNTER AGENCIES, AND INTERNAL RECRUITERS VERSUS JOB SERVICE AGENCIES

There are headhunters/recruiters and there are job service providers/agencies. It is important to understand the difference. The former is free, the latter will charge you for their services.

Recruiting/Headhunters Agencies

Recruiting agencies/headhunters should NEVER ask for you to pay for their service because the hiring company is paying them to find you. They receive their payment/commission on the back side after you have been hired. They are a third-party company and their fees are negotiated with the contracting/hiring company and is typically based on a percentage from your final negotiated annual salary. Therefore, they are working for you to ensure you get the highest possible salary…the more you make when you start, the more they make on their commission for finding you. Conduct your due diligence when using a recruiting agency – some are better than others. Also, ask questions-lots of questions-to determine if this agency is a good fit for you and your goals. Some recruiting agencies are industry and/or geographically specific.

Internal Company Recruiters

Internal company recruiters should NEVER ask for you to pay for their service **because they work for the company looking to hire you**. That is their job with the company, to find talented professionals qualified to work for their company and to fill their company's open job requisitions. Keeping that in mind, they work for that company and therefore are trying to get you to join their company at the most cost effective (low) rate that they can convince you to start work for. They may entice you with sign on bonuses and whatever else you can negotiate…get it all in writing, and READ AND UNDERSTAND THE CONTRACT THOROUGHLY BEFORE SIGNING. Some sign on bonuses and benefits are contingent upon retaining your employment for a minimum specified time. I have observed some companies offering great sign on bonuses only to cut/release/terminate the employee short of their contingent employment time frame and the employee ended up losing their entire sign on bonus.

Job Service Agencies

Job service agencies work for you. I DO NOT RECOMMEND USING JOB SERVICE AGENCIES. BUYER BE WARE. They WILL charge you, either up front or on the back sided after you get hired. They typically will have you sign a contract for a specified amount up front for their services (resume review, limited job searching, and interview preparation). These companies typically end up charging you several thousands of dollars over the course of several months. Some of these agencies even charge YOU a percentage of your new annual salary as a part of their fees. More times than not, they do not guarantee you will get a job, only that they can provide networking assistance to increase your opportunity for getting an interview.

Read Your Contract!

Whichever option you decide to work with, read over and fully understand your contract. If something is different or was left out or was added that you did not discuss, DO NOT SIGN IT. Verify your time off, bonuses, starting salary, benefits, and overall compensation package is what you discussed and agreed to in every detail. Only when everything looks right, then sign it. This may seem like a no brainer but you would be shocked (perhaps not) to learn how many people just sign paperwork without thoroughly reading, understanding, and verifying the information is correct. Do not be surprised if some companies try to rush you into signing paperwork – when this happens, take even more caution and care as it may be a red flag that something may be amiss in the paperwork.

15 RESUMES FOR YOUR TOOLBOX

There are several types of resumes you may/will need for your resume toolbox. Correct, you heard and understood…you will need more than one type of resume. Each has an intended purpose and use. The key thing here is to translate your military titles, jobs, and skills into easy to understand "normal" civilian terms. Also, do not use military acronyms (there are enough of those floating around in the civilian workplace to make the military list of acronyms seem like your weekly grocery list). Do not use military jargon in your descriptions either – translate them into the civilian language. Also, do not use abbreviations, spell everything out (great office wars have raged for years over misinterpreted abbreviations and acronyms). This means your descriptions may become a bit generic but at least they will be understandable to those who are not in the military. Finally, most employers in industry use various resume scanning software designed to identify potential candidates through a statistical algorithm – so ensure you are capturing key words from the job requisition in your resumes and cover letters. Below are brief descriptions of several types of resumes you will create and use.

Government Resume

This resume is used for applying to government jobs. USAJOBS contains information on what to include and what to leave out. Basically, you will include all your professional experience and education, to/from dates, salary, location, job title, salary, and other related information. You will leave out personally identifiable information (PII) such as your social security number, personal information (religion, gender, age, etc.), photos, and any classified or proprietary information. This is going to be a LONG resume, and intentionally so because you want to ensure it passes through the electronic scanning resume software. The potential benefit of this resume-opedia about you is that you can use it as the basis for all other resumes. These can typically be five to fifteen pages.

Detailed Resume

This resume is similar to, yet quite different from, the government resume. While detailed information about your qualifications is presented and quantified, it should be a significantly pared down version that is between two to five pages. You can use your government resume to help develop this resume or development this one separately.

Professional Resume

This resume can be parsed from your detailed resume. This is a higher level summary of your detailed resume and assimilates your experience categorically by primary skillset areas. This resume should be one to two pages in length.

Targeted Resume

This is a deliberate resume that can also be developed from your detailed resume. It is used to apply to a specific job requisition within a company. You will include key words, phrases, and statements from the job description to help identify you as a potential candidate. This resume is typically two to three pages.

Chronological Resume

I have found this type of resume to be somewhat outdated in its traditional method/form and somewhat ineffective. The detailed resume and targeted resume necessarily incorporate a chronology in their development. Traditionally, this is a very terse resume whereby your experience is listed chronologically. This resume is typically one to two pages in length.

Skill Based Resume

I have found this type of resume to be somewhat outdated in its traditional method/form and somewhat ineffective. The professional resume necessarily identifies work history under a list of skills in its development. Traditionally, this is a very terse resume whereby your experience is listed by relevant skills. This resume is typically one to two pages in length.

Cover Letters

Traditional Cover Letter

The traditional narrative style cover letter still has its uses. In industry, many companies have begun migrating away from traditional narrative style cover letter because of the wordiness and fluff that is used to fill blank space on the paper. That being said, some entities still use/prefer it, such as higher education (colleges and universities) and some health care facilities/institutions.

Professional Cover Letter

The professional cover letter is starting to become somewhat mainstream as it provides a short direct overview of what you are offering to the employer. When developed properly, you can use your professional resume as your professional cover letter – so you are getting a two for one there.

Part IV: Practical Tips for a Successful Transition

16. You are NEVER Alone in this Journey

17. What Do I Do Now?! – 22 Tips to Successful Career Positioning

18. Final Closing Thoughts

16 YOU ARE NEVER ALONE IN THIS JOURNEY

Seek out a mentor, coach, or colleague who has successfully navigated the transition to being a contributing member in the civilian sector.

Grow your professional network (e.g. LinkedIn). This will pay dividends on many levels. While the people in your immediate network may not be the ones to hire you, they may know someone who knows someone who knows someone who is looking for someone just like you. Never underestimate the power of a good network, they can be your eyes, ears, and voice for advancing and promoting your career and accomplishments.

Start/stay in college. I cannot over emphasize this topic enough. If you are not attending a four-year degree program from a regionally accredited college or university, START NOW. Just like having children or getting a puppy, there is never a perfect time…it is just something you commit to doing, and go do it. If you are already attending a four-year degree program from a regionally accredited college or university, STAY THE COURSE. If you have finished your undergraduate/Bachelor's degree, strongly consider starting a graduate/Master's program. Why? Because showing you are pursuing a Master's degree is better than just having a Bachelor's degree – it becomes a point of separation and distinguishes you from your competition. If you have Master's degree, consider pursuing a doctorate degree for the exact same reason. If you are one of the rare few that already has achieved a doctorate degree – in all seriousness, contact me! Attending college/university is an important way to keep yourself surrounded with like-minded people with the same/similar goals. It is also a valuable networking environment.

17 WHAT DO I DO NOW?! – 22 TIPS TO SUCCESSFUL CAREER POSITIONING

This final section offers 22 tips on how to successfully navigate into the civilian world and helps ensure proper career positioning. Do not try and reinvent the wheel, lean on and depend upon your support network of peers, colleagues, mentors, and coaches during this process. Are you ready? Here we go!

1.   Identify Your Transferable Skills

Make a list of your military skills in one column. In the next column describe your military skills in simpler terms; as if you were explaining then to a new troop just out of basic training or to a senior in high school – say it in terms they will understand.

2.   Create a Professional Skills Inventory

Once you have identified and translated your military skills into easy to understand words so simple a rock could understand, boil each description down into one to three simple summarized words that describe these skills. This will become your professional skills inventory. You can use this in your resume building, during interviews for describing what you did in the military, and to review and confirm you are developing the skills you want to expand. Whether you have all these skills or not, you now know what skills you need to build or those to improve.

3.   Reinvent Yourself

Use this opportunity to reinvent yourself. What does that mean, you may ask? Take the opportunity to work or do what you have always wanted to do. If you liked/loved what you did in the military – great, do that. If you wished you could do something different, now is your chance! Use this time to pursue your dream job in your dream location or start your own business. I am not saying it will be easy but you will be happy. My father has always told me "If you do what you love, the money, happiness, and success will follow."

4.   Create a Better Version of You…YOU2.0

If you liked/loved what you did in the military, seek out the next step in the continuum. Become a subject matter expert, get a certification, earn your next level higher college degree, start your own business. Take YOU to the next level!

5.   Develop a Plan

By this point you should have created a skills inventory (Tip 2) (in a language all us commoners can understand). You should also have an idea of what you want to do now that you are all grown up and out on your own. Now it is time to develop a plan. This may seem like a rather easy task, or conversely, a daunting task depending upon your perspective. Careful planning will become beneficial as you move forward. Sometimes we can get stuck in our own heads when developing our career plan. The simplest way to develop a plan is to start with the end in mind and move backward from your goal (in other words, reverse engineer your goal). Based on your list, you should have determined (or at least have an idea) of what you want to do now that you are out of the military. Think about your goal, then think about what needs to happen just prior to reaching that goal. Then think about and identify what needs to happen just before that, and so on. From this you will likely identify some things that you need to accomplish to achieve your overall plan. Then try to think about a couple "what if" scenarios, and how you would overcome those challenges. If needed, contact members of your network, colleagues, friends, mentors, coaches, etc. to help you develop your plan and alternate scenarios. After all, that is one of the reasons you have asked them for guidance or support.

6.   Stick to Your Plan; But be Willing to Modify

Your Plan if Needed

When you have developed your plan – stick to it. Just like in the military, trust your instincts and the signs around you. If it is your plan to cross a bridge but the bridge is out – adapt your plan and overcome the obstacle (over, under, around, through, across). Modifying your plan is all about perception and how you overcome challenges… and there will be challenges, my friend. Use your military finesse to creatively (legally) overcome the challenges you will be presented with. Embrace the suck; Pain is weakness leaving the body; What does not kill you makes you stronger; If it does not kill you, kill it instead; It is a character building experience…whatever it takes, you will overcome!

7.   Start and Stay in School; it Looks Good on a Resume, and Only Helps You

You are thinking "I know already…get/stay in school. I got the message first hundred times you said it in this book." Well, here it is again, start a four-year college program from a regionally accredited institution; complete your college program from your regionally accredited institution; pursue the next level of higher education – do not step down in a degree sequence. What I mean is, if you have a Master's degree, do not get another Bachelor's degree. Also, do not get a second degree at the same level unless it is required or unless you are changing career focus. Always pursue the next higher degree. In the same time it takes to get a second degree, you could have attained (or be close to attaining) the next higher degree. Do you want to say you have two Bachelor's degrees or a Master's degree? Do you want to say you have two Master's degrees or a Doctorate? Think about it. Reach out to me if you still have questions or doubts.

8.   Send Out Resumes Early

Start sending out your resumes four to six months prior to separation and/or receiving your college degree. This puts your name in the hands of potentially interested employers and recruiters. It also is a way to market yourself into a job by letting perspective employers know that you are getting close to completing your term and/or degree and you have a lot to offer. Some employers will actually start working with you early so they can bring you into the company immediately after you separate from the military and/or finish your degree.

9.   Remember Your Military Lessons

I am not talking about marksmanship (unless you are going into law enforcement) – although the principle of breath control may apply. I am talking about all the tough and easy lessons you learned that helped you hone your skills. I am talking about remembering what went well and repeating those lessons; and remembering what did not work out and why, and ensuring you do not repeat those mistakes. Remember all the blood, sweat, tears, tribulation, joy, and triumph …embrace and accept them. Let them be the fuel in your gut in a way that keeps you energized when things get tough…and the focus when things are going great.

10.   You Have More Skills Than You Realize

When remembering your military lessons, reflect on what skills you used (military or translated versions, it does not matter here because you are reflecting to yourself quietly and hopefully not out loud in line a fast food restaurant – awkward). Reflect on how you used those skills, when you used them, when you did not use them, and why you chose to use the skills you did when you did. These skills are your assets and value. You own these skills, they are yours – forever. Any good prospective employer will appreciate them the way you do (once you translate them into terms they will understand, of course).

11.   Keep   your   Military   Bearing   and Professionalism – it Separates You in a Good Way From "Normal" Civilians

Want to grow your hair out in dreds, gauge your earlobes, tattoo your face, and get a nose piercing? I would challenge you to think twice before going too far (unless you goal is to work in a tattoo shop, then go for it). You can do what you want, I am just saying to think about it before you follow through. Your military bearing, professionalism, and presentation go beyond skin deep – this too is an asset. It is how you present yourself to colleagues, friends, supervisors, co-workers, associates, and other professionals. Things such as standing up straight, speaking clearly, dressing properly for the event/job, being respectful (even when others are not necessarily being respectful to you) should not be taken for granted – they separate you in a good way as a professional.

12.   Be Humble and Confident, not Arrogant

While in the military, we learned, and became accustomed to, rank having its benefits. We also became accustomed to being able to "direct" others on what to do, when to do it, and how to do it. This is a good leadership skill; however, we must remember to always be confident yet humble, and never arrogant. There can be a fine line between confidence and arrogance – learn the difference, skirt the line but do not cross over into arrogance. In the military, arrogance can be cockiness can have its place. However, arrogance and cockiness in the civilian environment is a no-go. If you combine humility with confidence, then you will come off as appreciative yet respectful.

13.   Show Them How Your Skills Translate

Now that you have a complete understanding (okay, maybe not totally complete) of how your military skills translate, you need to show employers how your skills translate and benefit them. Ask questions that help you understand their needs, then discuss and show them how your skills, experience, and education could address these needs. Doing this will show that you not only understand their needs but that you know how to use and apply your skills to bring value to them and to their organization.

14.   Speak in Non-Military Language and Terms
       – it Takes Practice

Whether showing them through discussion or through example, remember to speak "civilian" with the interviewer. Even if they are known to be prior military. Sometimes prior military become institutionalized to their new workplaces and forget how to speak military because they have been immersed in a civilian work environment. To be accepted, they too must adapt (just as you will, over time) to the nuances of various civilian work place environments.

15.   Be Patient With Yourself and Others

Hurry up and wait…the first lesson we learned aside from how to do a proper push up. As military/prior military, we know a thing or two about patience. Learning to be a civilian will take time; weeks, months, perhaps even years (as in my case). It is okay if it takes a while, it just means you adapted well to one of the most challenging societal environments. Learning new habits takes time, and immersion is a great tool to help learn good habits. Think about it from a driving perspective…When you were overseas, how long did it take you to learn how to drive well in a different country with different laws? Perhaps you even had to learn how to drive on a different side of the road? Another example, how long did it take you to learn the nuances of the new command structure at your new base/installation? Not very long, right? Why are those easier than learning to be a civilian? They are not, there is no difference. It is about your perspective and expectations of yourself. So be patient with yourself, and others, as you transition.

16.   Alcohol Use

This is a sensitive topic to broach. If you do not drink alcohol, now is a good time to start – JUST KIDDING! If you drink alcohol, now is a good time to reduce your consumption.

Admittedly, most members of the military do have an adult alcohol-based beverage from time to time – it is almost a cultural element of the military. If you do imbibe in the occasional libation, please do so in moderation. Keep to the "not more than eight hours prior" rule. I am not suggesting for you to stop, rather merely asking you to consider moderating your consumption while you transition. If you do not drink alcohol, do not use this time as an excuse to start – it can become a very slippery slope that can lead to real problems and challenges that cannot be overcome by simply altering your perspective. Enough said, point made, I am now slowly walking away from this topic towards the door, with my back against the wall, no sudden moves, please. We are all still friends here, peace.

17.   Be Resilient, Persistent, Assertive, but Courteous

Be resilient – remember your military roots and grounding, they will serve you well. Be persistent – never stop, never let go, never give up: stay the course to your goal. Be assertive – go after what you want in tactful, respectful ways. Be courteous – kill them with kindness and respect; be respectful of their views and beliefs.

18.   Remain Calm

Calm and collected keeps a clear head; A cool head keeps a warm heart.

This is perhaps your greatest asset in the face of adversity. Remaining calm in frustrating and challenging situations allows us the benefit of awareness and clarity. The military has taught us, repeatedly, to stay calm, remain calm, and calm others. When people (and ourselves) are calm, we tend to be less reactive and more evaluative if the situation. Keeping a calm clear head has prevented many mistakes and lead to great successes. Remember, no matter how frustrated (or stressed in some cases) you may become, keep your head in a good place and keep your calm. Many wars and family disputes have been avoided by remaining calm and cool.

19.   The Military You Know/Remember no Longer Exists…it has Evolved, So Have You

The most significant lesson, and coincidentally the longest lesson, I learned about leaving the military was that the military I miss/love, no longer exists. It has not existed for many years, decades even. Within a few months after each separation, the military I knew and loved was already gone because the military is constantly evolving; faster than ever. Up through the late 1980's and into the early 1990's, the Cold War kept military cultural evolution fairly constant. Then the wall fell and the Cold War ended. Military culture started to slowly and incrementally change during the mid-1990's. By 2000, there was a marked difference between the military culture of the pre-1990's and the early 2000's. By the time I was discharged in 2003, there was a marked difference in the military culture from just three years prior. Now, military culture is morphing at a much higher pace, whereby military cultural change can be easily observed after just a few short months. Just as the military adapts and evolves, so do you. You have been adapting and evolving over your entire military career (whether long or short). Do not stop evolving now.

20.   Be Flexible – Change is Growth

Challenge yourself to be flexible, with yourself and others. This may mean you might have to change in some way shape or form. I know, I said the "C" word (change). Many people shy away from or are afraid or are simply unwilling to change. I challenge all those perspectives (and others) because life IS change. Change is growth. Change is life. If you had not "changed/grown" in the military, you would not have remained in the military. If you did not change your approach, attitude, perspective, perception, physical self, then you would still be the same exact person you were X number of years ago, before you entered the military. If you did not change your mindset, you would not have promoted or finished your technical training. If you had not been changing over the years, you would not be/have become the person you are today. Change is about growth; and to grow, implies to be flexible. There are several forms of flexibility. Flexible to learn and adapt. Flexible to be patient with yourself, your family, and your friends. Flexible with time and expectations and the path you have chosen. Flexible to alter your perspective to successfully overcome all challenges and achieve your goals. Remember, it/everything is ALWAYS about perspective.

21.   Positive and Optimistic About the Future

This one is not only about perspective but also about conscious choice. You choose your perspectives, no one else does. Therefore, choose to be optimistic. Would you confront a challenge by saying…"Well, I guess I am going to fail at this task" or "I am not going to do well at this job" or after watching many people successfully bungie jump say "I know everyone else has succeeded in this bungie jump but I am pretty sure my head is going to hit the ground". No, most assuredly you would not. The military has taught us to always be positive about facing challenges and overcoming them. If we confront a challenge with a positive outlook, we are more likely to overcome it and succeed in our goals. The same holds true about the challenge for transitioning from the military to becoming a civilian. This transition is your next adventure/journey/challenge. Embrace it with all the positive vigor you can muster and jump into the pool! – the water is only cold for a little while.

22.   Have Faith and Trust

Finally, and most importantly, have faith and trust: in yourself, your support system, your family and friends, your colleagues, your God(s), etc. This is your greatest team; your religion, spirituality, your training, your experience, and your education. This transition will not always be peaches and roses but it will be productive. You will change, grow, and adapt. You may not normally be comfortable depending on others however, YOU MUST BECOME COMFORTABLE LEANING ON YOUR SUPPORT SYSTEM (comfortable with, not dependent upon). You cannot do everything, all the time – that is a recipe for disaster. You will burn out. Use your faith and trust to overcome all obstacles. Use your faith and trust to empower you. Use your faith and trust to succeed. You can do this; you WILL do this! You will overcome this challenge just as you have overcome hundreds of other challenges throughout your life. Remember, above all else, it is always about your perspective; and your perspective will dictate your success.

18 FINAL CLOSING THOUGHTS

Congratulations! You are now prepared to take on and successfully overcome the military transition challenge. I have used and shared these principles and concepts over the past 15 years to help hundreds of transitioning military, veterans, and civilians to successfully position their careers. The one constant I found over and over was that, experientially, career transitioning is the same no matter who you are. I have realized it was less about the transition itself and more about having the proper perspectives and positioning yourself well for a new career. It is never too late. Remember to engage all those that support you and your efforts. I hope you have found solace in knowing you are never alone in this journey. I also hope that you have found value in the wisdom and tips discussed, along with inspiration from experiences shared in these pages. God Spede in all you do and strive to achieve.

ABOUT THE AUTHOR

Dr. Dave Peltz, Founder and President of Peltz Consulting Services, is a leadership and adult learning subject-matter expert who provides career positioning coaching services for civilians and military members. Dr. Peltz also teaches undergraduate and graduate studies in the areas of business, leadership, research, and statistics.

He attributes his knowledge, experience, and business acumen to three career phases: military and civilian law enforcement; corporate defense manufacturing; and leadership/business consulting. These three distinct and very different phases have provided him with detailed insights on change and adapting to extreme or opposing environments. His experiences have enabled him to efficiently comprehend challenging situations and develop effective solutions through innovation and foresight.

Dr. Peltz has received numerous team and individual awards and recognitions throughout his career. He has also given numerous presentations, nationally and internationally, on topics such as servant leadership, human resource development, and adult learning.

He holds a Doctorate of Philosophy (PhD) in Organizational Leadership with a major in Human Resource Development from Regent University; Master's in Business Administration (MBA) with a specialization in Global Management from the

University of Phoenix; and a Bachelor's of Science degree with a major in Business Management from the University of Phoenix. He also has several industry related certifications.

Email: peltzcs@outlook.com
Twitter: @drdavepeltz
Website: www.dpeltzphd.com
LinkedIn: www.linkedin.com/in/david-peltz-ph-d-84297b18

DR. DAVID P. PELTZ

CONTACT INFORMATION

Dr. Peltz offers a variety of services on Career Positioning topics contained in this text to include: seminars, presentations, workshops, trainings, coaching, and mentoring.

Please feel free to reach out to Dr. Peltz with any questions, comments, or stories you would like to share.

Dr. Peltz is best contacted via email at: peltzcs@outlook.com

REFERENCES

Agile. www.icagile.com/

Bayt. www.bayt.com/

CareerBuilder. www.careerbuilder.com/

Certified Professional Property Manager (CPP-various). www.npma.org/

Deci, E. L. (1975). Intrinsic Motivation. New York, NY: Plenum Press.

Deci, E. L., & Ryan, R. M. (1985). Intrinsic motivation and self-determination in human behavior. New York, NY: Plenum.

Glassdoor. www.glassdoor.com/

HigherEdJobs. www.higheredjobs.com/

Indeed. www.indeed.com/

Industrial and/or Contract Property Management (ICPM-various). www.dau.mil/

Institutionalize. (2011). *American Heritage Dictionary of the English Language* (5th ed). Retrieved from http://www.thefreedictionary.com/institutionalize

Lean. www.asq.org/

Lean Six Sigma. www.iassc.org/

Lean Startup. www.theleanstartup.com/

LinkedIn. www.linkedin.com/

List of Online Colleges with Regional Accreditation. (2017). Guide to Online Schools.com. Retrieved from http://www.guidetoonlineschools.com/resources/accreditation/regional-accreditation?page=

Monster. www.monster.com/

Perception. (2010). *Random House Kernerman Webster's College Dictionary*. Retrieved from http://www.thefreedictionary.com/perception

Perspective. (2014). *Collins English Dictionary – Complete and Unabridged*, (12th ed.). (1991, 1994, 1998, 2000, 2003, 2006, 2007, 2009, 2011, 2014). Retrieved from http://www.thefreedictionary.com/perspective

Positioning. (2011). *American Heritage® Dictionary of the English Language*, (5th ed). Retrieved from www.thefreedictionary.com/positioning

Professional in Human Resources. www.hrci.org/

Program Management Professional. www.pmi.org/

Project Management Professional. www.pmi.org/

Regional Accreditation vs National Accreditation for Online Colleges. (2017). GetEducated.com. Retrieved from http://www.geteducated.com/regional-vs-national-accreditation-which-is-better-for-online-colleges

Reis, E. (2011). The Lean Startup: How Today's Entrepreneurs Use Continuous Innovation to Create Radically Successful Businesses. New York, NY: Crown Business.

SHRM Certified Professional. www.shrm.org/

Six Sigma. www.asq.org/

TheLadders. www.theladders.com/

USAJOBS. www.usajobs.gov/

VirtualVocations. www.virtualvocations.com/

Vroom, V. H. (1964). Work and Motivation. New York, NY: John Wiley & Sons Inc.

www.ingramcontent.com/pod-product-compliance
Lightning Source LLC
Chambersburg PA
CBHW061440180526
45170CB00004B/1490